BROOKLYN IN THE SIXTIES
Photographs by Howard B. Jurgrau

Foreword by T. J. Galler

CRANE & HOPPER
PUBLISHERS

Acknowledgments:

To Barbara Caldwell of Prospect Park Alliance; Lori Duggan Gold of Brooklyn Botanic Garden; Fran Hackett of New York Aquarium, and Alison Power of Central Park Zoo for the information contained in the captions.

To Dr. Victor Burnett and St. John's Episcopal Hospital for permission to use photos on pages 89-92.

To Robert Zagby for permission to use two photos on pages 40-41, and to Martin A. Ralston for permission to use the photo of Howard B. Jurgrau on the back cover.

To Claire Angelica for help with publicity.

Brooklyn in the Sixties
Photographs by Howard B. Jurgrau

Copyright 1995 by Crane & Hopper.
All rights reserved.
Published by Crane & Hopper
P.O. Box 234
Chappaqua, New York 10514

Book design by Bernadette Evangelist, Robert Anthony, Inc., New York City.

First published 1995
10 9 8 7 6 5 4 3 2 1

Library of Congress Cataloging-in-Publication Data

Brooklyn in the sixties / photographs by Howard B. Jurgrau : foreword
   by T. J. Galler.
      p. cm.
   ISBN 0-9640977-4-5 (pbk.)
   1. Brooklyn (New York, N.Y.)—Social life and customs—Pictorial
works. 2. New York (N.Y.)—Social life and customs—Pictorial
works. I. Jurgrau, Howard B., 1925–1972.
F129.B7B746 1995
974.7'23043—dc20   95–16752
                                                                 CIP

PRINTED IN HONG KONG

Photo on front cover taken at Bailey Fountain, Grand Army Plaza.

Table of Contents

	Page
Foreword	5
Botanic Garden	9
Water Sports	19
The Zoo	29
Parkside Avenue	39
Prospect Park	51
The Aquarium	71
Coney Island	79
St. John's Episcopal Hospital	89
About the Photographer	95

For Robert, Andrea, and Maura

Foreword

Many young people today look back with longing to the Sixties as a time when youth embraced certain ideals and took action to pursue them: when students demanded and got the right to plan their own education, when they supported the cause of integration and went to jail for it, when they protested against the Vietnam War and stopped it, and when they resisted the draft by leaving the country. Too, the Sixties bring to mind visions of personal freedom: a time when you could scream your head off at a rock concert; bend and twist your body to the heavy beat with others in the crowd; take a long toke on a joint before passing it to your friends; become a member of a commune where you could cultivate the land or meditate; or thumb your way to the West Coast, call yourself a flower child, and live from day to day.

The Sixties' thrust toward liberation was real enough, reflecting a worldwide impulse toward political change. Africa reverberated with cries for independence. Students rioted in Paris, Regensburg, Tokyo, Rome, Madrid, Buenos Aires, Rio de Janeiro, among other cities throughout the world, often with the support of their teachers, against established authorities that were seen as stifling or conservative. In the U.S., the liberals had once again assumed the leadership of the Federal Government, signalling an end to the repressive McCarthy Era and a hope for greater social equality, especially through the enforcement of the Civil Rights Laws enacted in the Fifties.

However, those who lived through the Sixties are bound to remember the fear and trembling that accompanied the sense of liberation. Kennedy defeats Nixon in 1960 only to be assassinated three years later, an act of terror repeated twice more before the decade is out, when Robert Kennedy and Martin Luther King are murdered. The Cold War between the Soviet Union and the U.S. escalates in spite of the change in U.S. administration and the fact that both nations are exploring outer space. The younger population is burgeoning due to the baby boom of two earlier decades, while the elderly are living longer with the help of medical science, looking askance at the antics of youth. While schools are being integrated, classrooms are overcrowded, and a debate rages over whether prayer should be allowed in the public schools. Police, national guard, and firemen are called out not only to enforce Civil Rights Laws, but also to break up peaceful demonstrations against the Vietnam War and to control exuberant audiences at rock concerts.

New York City enters the Sixties with its reputation intact as leader in commerce and finance for the continent. There is a dramatic spurt in skyscraper construction dwarfing the building boom of the Twenties. Planning for the '64/'65 World's Fair in Queens is begun; a world trade center is proposed for lower Manhattan to serve the expanding needs of international commerce; new schools are opened and others are planned; Leonard

Bernstein conducts the Gloria from Beethoven's *Missa Solemnis* at the opening of the first unit of Lincoln Center, Philharmonic Hall, in 1962.

In Brooklyn, work continues on the Verrazano-Narrows Bridge to connect Brooklyn and Staten Island, but the beginning of the decade is marred by two disasters: the jet airliner crash into Sterling Place, killing 128 people, and the fire on the aircraft carrier Constellation at the Brooklyn Navy Yard, killing 49. Of the five boroughs, Brooklyn benefits least from the general prosperity of the city. In fact, many neighborhoods are losing their middle class population to the suburbs as a result of racial integration. The phenomenon known as "redlining," where real estate brokers try to scare home owners into selling their property, abets this population shift.

The black population becomes more militant in its fight for decent housing and education, especially after the assassination of Martin Luther King in April of 1968. New York City teachers go on strike for five weeks in the fall of that year, in a dispute involving an experiment in community control at Ocean Hill-Brownsville, where the community attempted to remove some of the white teachers. Since many teachers are Jewish, the strike takes on religious as well as racial overtones. Thus tension mounts during this decade in a way that makes Brooklyn a microcosm of the world, filled with hope for the future, yet fearful of the turmoil that accompanies profound social change.

The photographs that follow are not directly illustrative of world events. Howard Jurgrau was not a photojournalist by profession, but he was a dedicated photographer who educated himself by reading, observing, and taking pictures. Having a technical bent, he learned all about the available equipment for producing black-and-white photographs. He studied the work of earlier photographers, especially that of Ansel Adams and Henri Cartier-Bresson—the former for his startling renderings of nature though sophisticated use of light filters and darkroom techniques; the latter for the dramatic image he produced in pursuit of the "decisive moment" during some human situation that was unfolding before his eyes.

Attending The Family of Man exhibition at the Museum of Modern Art in New York in 1955, where 500 photographs from all over the world displayed people in typical human endeavor, Howard Jurgrau recognized that photography had the capacity to blend technology and art in the service of humanity and that photographs could unite people in a way that other forms of communication had so far been unable to—by showing their essential similarity. He was also affected by the revised concept of the decisive moment, exemplified in Robert Frank's *The Americans* (1959), a photographic collection of seemingly chance glimpses of life in the U.S.

The photographs by Howard Jurgrau contained in this book are mostly of people involved in activities more or less usual at half a dozen outdoor sites in Brooklyn and at two or three indoor ones. To the extent that they portray people in ordinary situations, the pictures express the photographer's vision of human connectedness as well as his desire to mirror the everydayness of life.

On the other hand, they also embody the way Brooklyn was a social and political miniature of the world at large: the expanding population of all ages especially the young, the tensions that accompany a city's efforts to integrate different generations and races, the desire of people to relate through music and dance, the ambiance of action and movement that may break out in rebellion or settle into brooding stillness. Subtler are the signs of change visible in body language, clothing and hair styles, and interior decoration—from the conventional mode of the Fifties to the informal one of the Sixties—that accompanied the sensational events.

Jurgrau's style is epitomized by a lack of artistic pretension. His eye is trained on the subject, his aim a factual picture. Paradoxically, a strong identification with the subject helped him achieve objectivity. Though the majority of his pictures show people in some form of activity rather than at rest, there are occasional landscapes or portraits in which the photographer has allowed his sympathy to emerge and where the appeal of the photograph lies rather in the pervasive mood than in the dynamics of movement. His view is always at eye-level with the subject, hardly ever from below, and never from above—certainly a confirmation of the ease with which he confronted other people and of his personal vision of the equality of all human beings. Such a vision was very much in keeping with the idealism of the Sixties and made Jurgrau a photographer of and for his time.

Rose Arc Pool

Botanic Garden

Magnolia Plaza in front of the Administration Building

Japanese Garden and Viewing Pavillion

Fragrance Garden

Cherry Walk

Terminal Pond

Jenkins Fountain on Lily Pool Terrace

Wollman Memorial Rink

Water Sports

Prospect Lake

Boating on Prospect Lake at Wollman Memorial Rink

Prospect Lake

View of Brooklyn Bridge from South Street Seaport

Dingo statues flanking the former entrance to the Zoo

The Zoo

Black rhinoceros

Arabian camel

African Elephant

African Lion

Tiger

Raccoon

Baboon

Sun bear

American Bison

Parkside Avenue

Buckminster Fuller's geodesic dome adapted for children

Photo by Robert Zagby

Photo by Robert Zagby

The Peristyle

Prospect Park

Near the Pergola entrance at Parkside and Ocean Avenues

Prospect Lake looking toward the Concert Grove

Ocean Avenue playground

Dancing at Wollman Memorial Rink

Ice-skating on Wollman Memorial Rink

Formerly the logo at the entrance to the Aquarium

The Aquarium

Pacific walrus in the Walrus Pool

Black-footed penguins in the Penguin Rookery

Feeding the white-sided dolphin

Beluga whale in the Polar Bay

Near the Penguin Rookery: Brightwater Tower buildings in the background

Formerly the Aquarium Tri-pool which housed harbor and grey seals

Coney Island

St. John's Episcopal Hospital

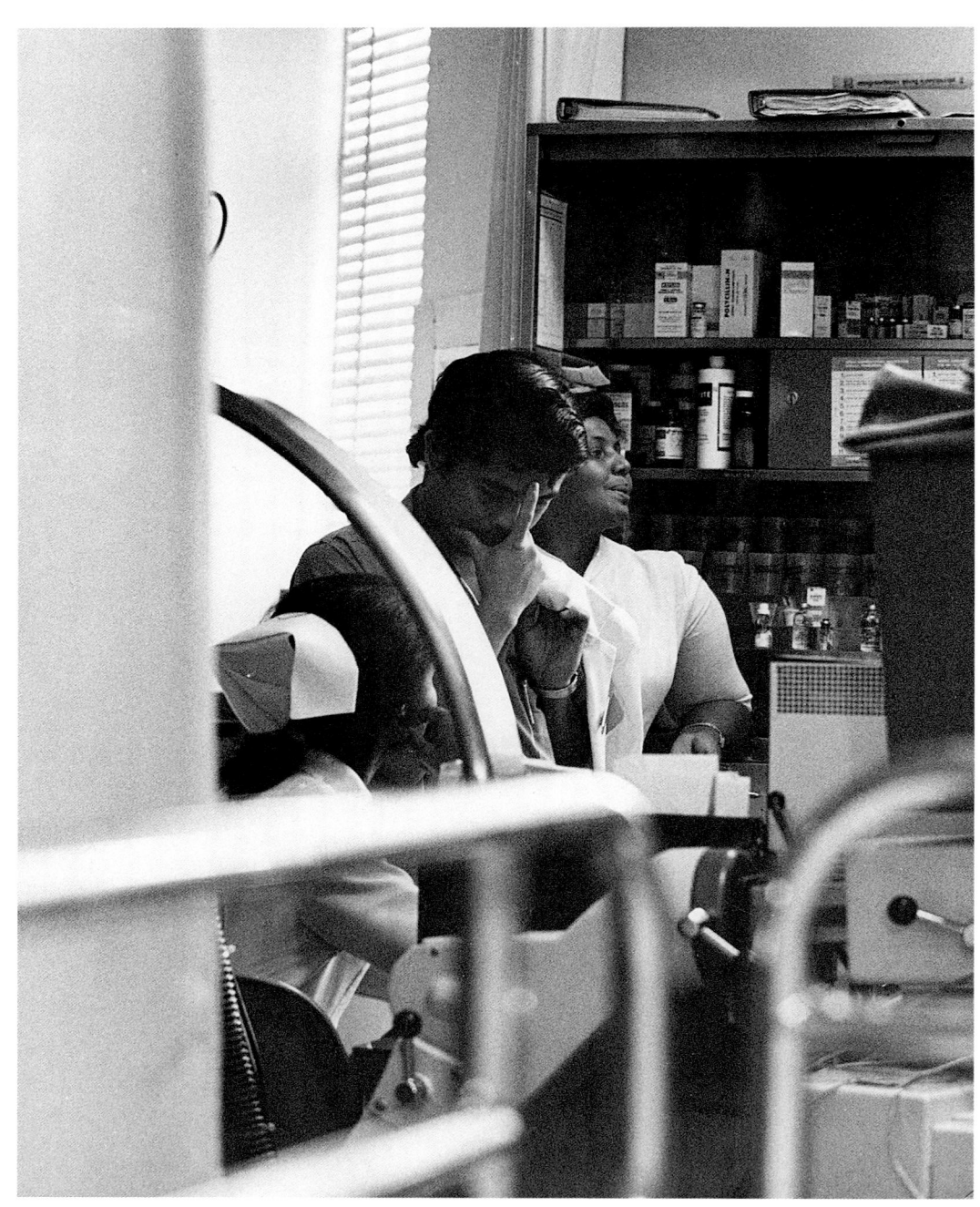

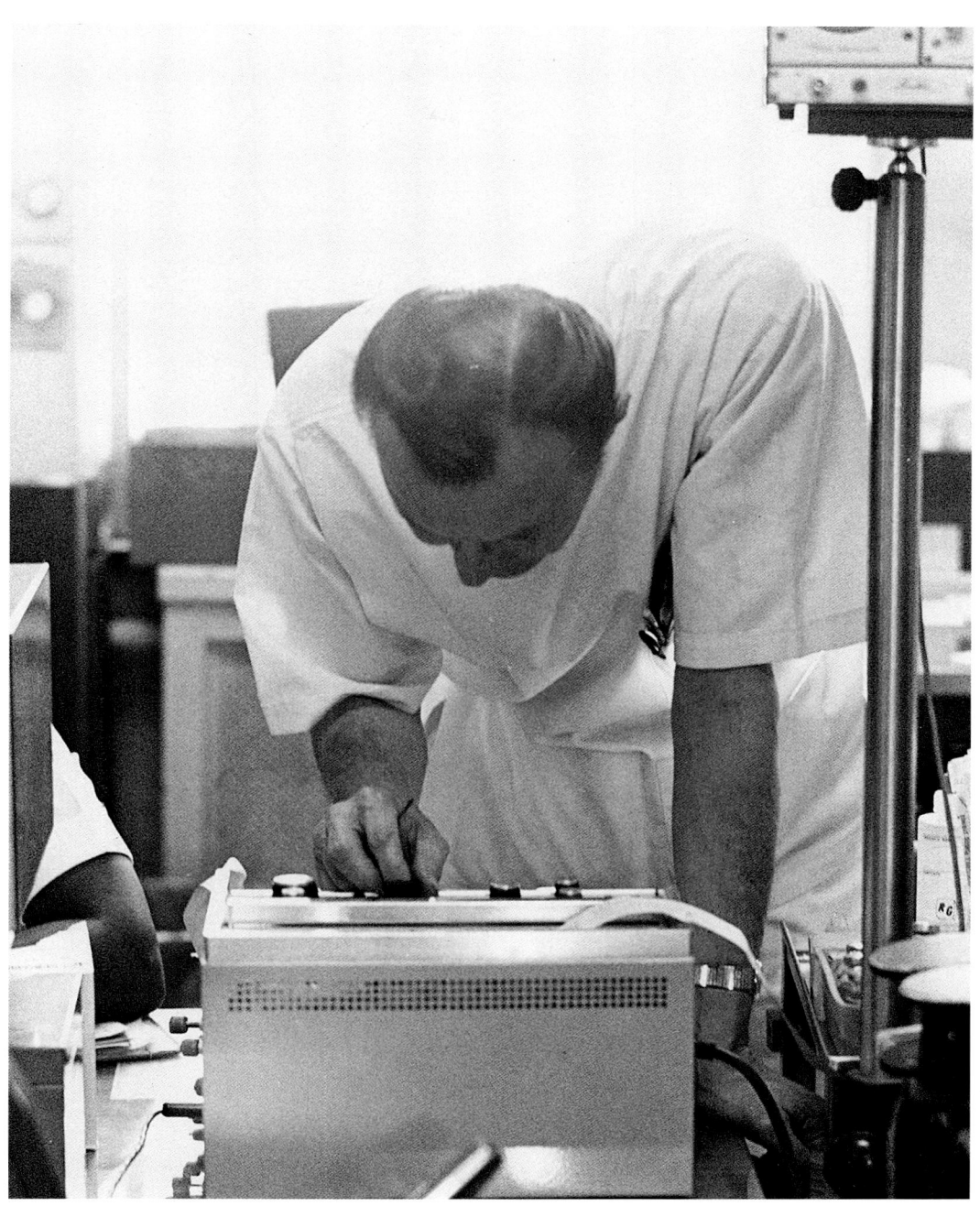

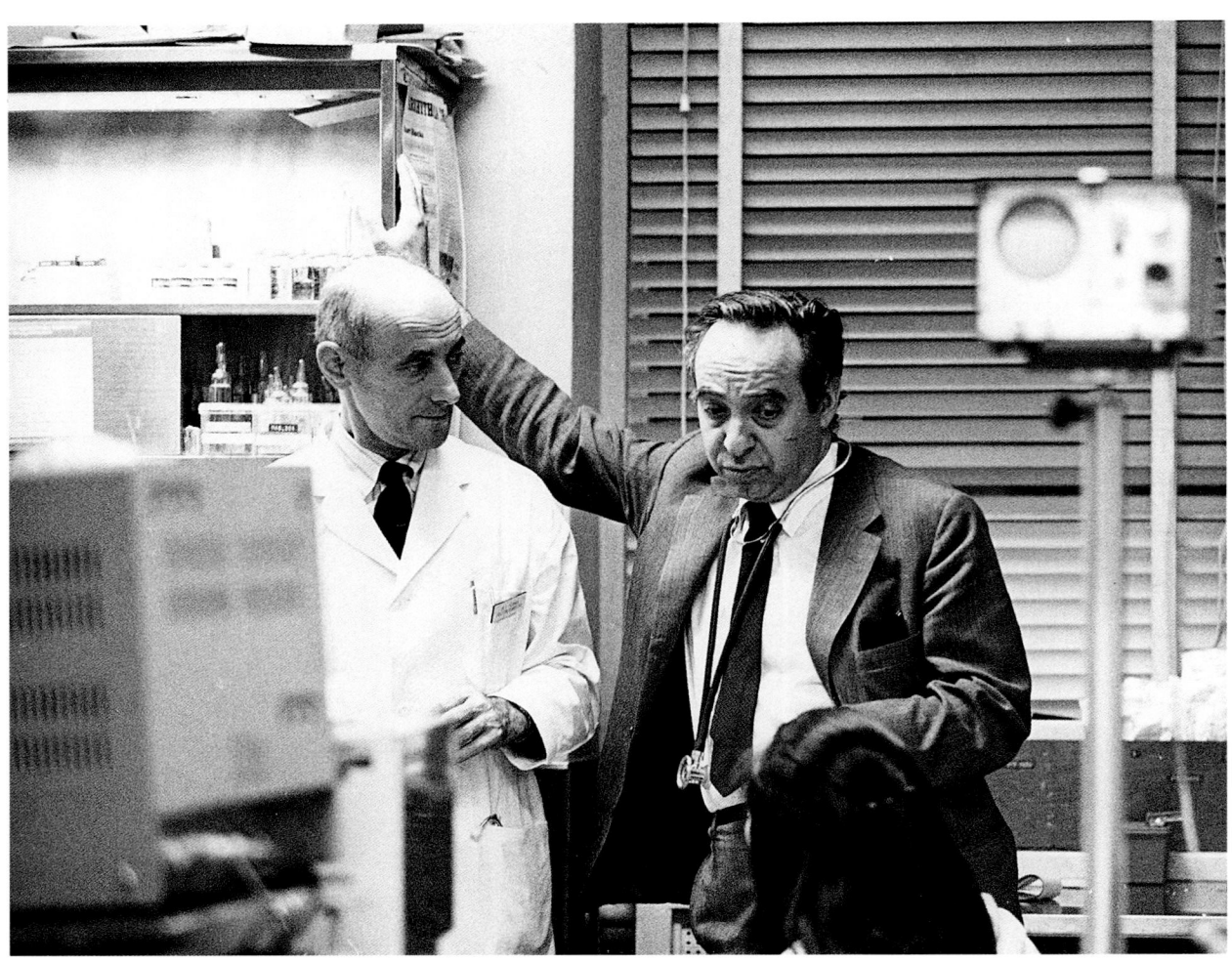

About the Photographer

Howard Jurgrau had a penchant for science. He was educated as a chemist and made a living selling technical equipment to labs and hospitals. Personally though, he gravitated toward artists: he felt that somehow their lives were more meaningful. His own creative urge was dormant until a writer friend suggested photography. Once he started taking pictures, he didn't stop.

Such had been the case with his many interests from childhood on—stamps, coins, dogs, cats, birds, tropical fish; once involved, he quickly became an expert. When he took to photography, he bought the best equipment, cleaned his lenses regularly, read the magazines of the trade, learned the jargon, paid daily visits to the camera store, and soon had several cronies with whom he could talk shop. Of course, he perused the books of those whose work he admired. His cameras became part of his wardrobe. Indoors and out, at least one was suspended by a strap from his neck, along with a bag on his shoulder containing equipment to cope with any eventuality of lighting or weather.

No one in the house on Parkside Avenue was safe from his inquisitive eye. His photographs of parties on the block show the diminishing formality from early to late Sixties. But the sights of Brooklyn became his preferred subject. He would go off with a bunch of kids—his and a few of the neighbors'—on trips to Prospect Park, the Zoo, Botanic Garden, Coney Island, ever scanning the scene for likely shots, while the children amused themselves.

His "hobby" lasted ten years, for he died of lymphosarcoma in 1972. The illness did not extinguish his photographer's zeal: witness the final pictures in this book, taken from a hospital bed. Thus, he amassed a portfolio of pictures of Brooklyn that caught the spirit of the decade. Rarely did he take a picture that didn't contain a person or an animal, for living creatures were his trademark, and their energy, in movement or at rest, adds to his pictures' interest more than thirty years later.